CW00487192

FRANK SINATRA

A Life from Beginning to End

Table of Contents

Introduction

One of the greatest American singers of all time, Francis Albert Sinatra, was born on December 12, 1915. His parents—Antonino Martino (better known as "Marty") and Natalina (known as "Dolly") Sinatra—had immigrated from Italy prior to his birth and set down roots in Hoboken, New Jersey.

This future megastar was a big baby, clocking in at a hearty thirteen and a half pounds (6.1 kilograms). Due to the heft of baby Sinatra, it was difficult for his then 19-year-old mother to give birth to him. Frank was being birthed at home with the help of a midwife, but once it became clear that it was not going to be an easy birth, a local doctor was summoned to assist. The doctor had with him a pair of forceps to aid in the process. Even with forceps applied, however, Frank still had a rough time of it, and the procedure itself would leave him scarred for life.

In later years, some might have noticed the scars on Sinatra's cheek and neck and assumed he received them from his rough-and-tumble days running the streets of Hoboken. But no—Frank Sinatra received these scars on his very day of birth due to the difficulty entailed in bringing him into this world. In truth, "Ol' Blue Eyes" was born entirely blue, suffering from a clear case of cyanosis; he wasn't even breathing. Upon pulling him out, the doctor had practically given up on him and placed the seemingly lifeless child next to a nearby sink while he tended to his barely conscious teenage mother. When someone eventually smacked little Frank on the back, the baby finally filled its lungs with air and began to cry.

Frank Sinatra had it tough from the very beginning it seems, but nevertheless, no matter what difficulties life had in store for him,

Sinatra always had a readymade plan to overcome them.

Chapter One

Early Life in Hoboken

"May you live to be a hundred, and may the last voice you hear be mine."

—Frank Sinatra

Sinatra was an inquisitive child, and from a young age, he was up and ready to explore the world. His mother, who led a busy lifestyle, had a more or less hands-off approach in his formative years. Dolly Sinatra was politically active in her community and often served as an interpreter for fellow immigrants. She also frequently worked as a midwife, helping to deliver babies. Frank Sinatra would later claim that he was primarily reared by a neighbor of the family, Mrs. Golden, a lady that Sinatra many years later would fondly remember as a "kindly Jewish woman" and his sweet "Yiddish Mommie."

Rolling around Hoboken as a youth, Frank felt slightly disadvantaged since he was an only child. He didn't have a big brother or big sister to look out for him; he was on his own. Neighbors would later recall many afternoons of Frank simply sitting outside his parents' house perched on his bicycle, all by his lonesome, waiting for his mother and father to come home.

His parents were indeed busy. Marty Sinatra was an amateur boxer before his injuries led him to retire. He then picked up work on the docks loading ships, a grueling enterprise. Frank's mother, in the meantime, had gotten in good with local politicians due to her ability to turn out locals to the polls on election day and was rewarded for her efforts. It was thanks to her growing connections that she was able to pull enough strings to get Marty a job at the Hoboken Fire Department. The pay raise Marty gained was enough to allow the family to move up-town to a nice apartment on Park Avenue.

Frank was 12 years old at the time of this big move. He was just starting junior high and considering what his future might bring. He must have felt a little self-conscious during the transition, but his mother always tried to give him confidence. She primarily did this by buying him a whole wardrobe of brand-new clothes. Compared to his peers, Frank was always the most well-dressed kid on the block. It's said that Frank was often ridiculed for his well-heeled appearance, just as easily as he was admired. Nevertheless, even at this young age, Frank Sinatra couldn't help but want to stand out.

Chapter Two

Struggling to Find His Way

"I'm not one of those complicated, mixed-up cats. I'm not looking for the secret to life. I just go on from day to day, taking what comes."

—Frank Sinatra

Frank Sinatra finished up his stint at Hoboken Junior High School in June of 1931. Nowadays, graduating from middle school isn't really considered a big deal, but back in the 1930s, having an eighth-grade education was still considered a momentous occasion.

Frank, like so many others of his peers, would ultimately end his schooling here. He tried attending the local high school, but after a little over a month, he left. It's not clear if he dropped out or was kicked out, but he was around 15 years old at the time of this academic departure.

Some accounts say that his mother was angry with him for ditching high school, but others reason that she was more pragmatic and simply assumed that he would find a job and join the workforce. She was definitely instrumental in getting him his first gig. It certainly wasn't glamorous, but after talking with a man she knew at a local paper called the *Jersey Observer*, she managed to get Frank hired to bundle newspapers and load them up in a newspaper delivery vehicle. The man who got him the job was a long-time family friend, Frank Garrick.

Sinatra quickly grew disenchanted with this form of manual labor, however, and he soon found an opportunity to extricate himself from it. The newsroom had received the tragic news that one of their writers had died in a car accident. Incredibly enough, Sinatra went right into the office of the deceased writer and began to pretend that he was filling in for him. Frank didn't really know how to write, but he proceeded to do all of the other things that he thought a writer might do. It's said he spent an inordinate amount of time sharpening pencils and shuffling papers. Obviously, he wouldn't be able to keep up this ridiculous routine forever, and soon enough, the editor inquired as to who he was and what he thought he was doing.

It was upon being questioned that Frank Sinatra lied and claimed that it was old Frank Garrick who had given him the new position. The editor, of course, went right over to Garrick and asked him about it. Garrick wasn't about to play along with Sinatra's game and informed the editor that

Sinatra was lying. The editor then told Garrick to terminate Sinatra's employment immediately. It's said that Garrick tried to let Sinatra down gently, but all the same, the boy lost it and began screaming and shouting at Garrick in the worst possible way. You would think that Sinatra might be thankful that Garrick got him the job and ashamed of himself for messing it up, but instead, he took his anger out on his benefactor.

This incident shows Sinatra's potential for volatile behavior, and when he went home and informed his mother of what had happened, she too indulged in holding a grudge against Garrick.

It's said that from there on out, the old family friend Frank Garrick was completely snubbed by both Sinatra and his mother. According to Garrick, Sinatra "called me every terrible name in the book, and then he stormed out. He never said another word to me until fifty years later, after his mother died."

At any rate, Dolly was determined to move up in the world, and in December of 1931, she moved the family into a large house near the Hudson. The home was said to have had four stories and plenty of room, and Dolly ultimately had to rent some of the rooms out to pay for it. Frank was at this time often not much more than a freeloader, and his mother was sure to periodically remind him of that fact.

It was at the insistence of his mother that Sinatra eventually got a job out on at the dockyards in Hoboken. Here, he worked on a freighter that shipped fruit, and his main task was to take out condenser units, clean them up, and put them back. This task he did, over and over on long, tedious shifts. It was during this monotonous work that his mind would often wander to what it might be like to do something different. Thinking back to all the time he had spent back home listening to early crooners on the radio such as Bing Crosby, that something different oftentimes centered around singing.

In his off time, Sinatra began hanging out with local musicians, and occasionally they would let him sing to their arrangements. His parents generally indulged Frank at this point and were said to allow him and his musical friends to practice in the basement of the family home. Still, Dolly would at times grow impatient with her son's chosen passion in life, and on at least one occasion, it was recalled how she shouted that he was a "bum" and threw one of her shoes at him. The most serious shock was still to come, however, when Frank Sinatra's father decided to throw him out of the house outright.

Chapter Three

Frank's First Love

"Whatever else has been said about me personally is unimportant. When I sing, I believe. I'm honest."

—Frank Sinatra

It was around 1934 when a teenage high school dropout without any real job prospects and not much of an outlook on his future—Frank Sinatra—was suddenly booted out of his parents' house. According to Frank's recollection, his mother was in tears as his usually mild-mannered father made this resolute decision and pointed to the door and said, "Get out." Sinatra then packed a suitcase and hopped on the Hoboken Ferry, heading to New York.

It's not exactly clear what Frank did during this time, but it seems that it was during this first expulsion from the family home that he first made a serious effort to make it big in music. Sinatra, after all, would later famously sing in his song "New York, New York" how if one could make it big there, then they could "make it anywhere." The harsh realities of trying to make it big hit Sinatra pretty quickly, and soon enough, he was back at his parents' door, much more compliant than he was before. His mother and father, perhaps encouraged by his newfound humility, welcomed him back with open arms. Not only that, but Frank apparently managed to convince his parents of how serious he was about wanting to become a singer.

His mother, for one, believed enough in her son to fork over $65 to purchase Sinatra his first professional microphone. That was a lot of money during the Great Depression when many others were struggling just to get enough food to eat or to keep a roof over their heads. All the same, having his own microphone was a major step in Frank Sinatra's career. It not only allowed him to practice at home, with his own practice amp, but more importantly, it allowed him to be heard when he dared to perform in front of an audience.

Today, just about every bar, pub, and coffee shop has its own sound system, and any budding performer at an open mic night will be handed a microphone, but back in the 1930s, microphones were a much rarer commodity. Prior to being gifted this microphone, the few times that Frank Sinatra tried to sing with a big band at a club, he had to sing as loudly as he possibly could just to be heard. Such a daunting task was not only cumbersome but also held a good chance of causing a singer to throw their voice out. Now, with his microphone in hand, Sinatra was able to croon as softly as he wanted while still able to fill up the room with his voice.

Even more helpful to Frank, his mother helped him get a used car, which proved immensely useful in hauling around his musical cohorts and their musical equipment. Soon Sinatra was regularly playing wherever he could, whether it was a local pub, a social hall, or even a high school dance—he was ready and willing to entertain.

He was also ready to have some fun. Riding high on his new exploits in music, a then 19-year-old Sinatra gave himself a bit of a vacation that summer of 1934 and headed over to the Jersey Shore to stay with his Aunt Josie, Dolly's sister. Spending his days relaxing and wandering around the beach, he also made some time to fall in love. It was that summer that Sinatra met a girl who lived just across the street from Aunt Josie, the 17-year-old Nancy Barbato.

It was apparently Frank who first caught Nancy's eye. She would sit on her porch and watch the giddy and recently tanned visitor as he made his way to the beach to soak up more sunshine. Frank would then see her lounging on her porch, seated in a wicker rocking chair, filing away at her nails, pretending she didn't notice him as he came and went. Nancy was interested in Frank from the beginning, but she was hardly going to just run up to him to strike up a conversation. If their relations were going to go any further than furtive glances, it would be up to Frank to make the first move, and he did so in the way that suited him best—through music.

Hoping to catch the girl's eye on one of those sunny days, Sinatra ventured out of his aunt's home with a ukulele in hand. Strumming a few simple chords, he boldly sang a song right there out in the open. Now, it would be impossible for Nancy to pretend she didn't notice him. Not only that but soon all of her sisters and cousins who had been inside the house were heading out to listen to Frank as well. Once his song was over, Sinatra was able to strike up a conversation with Nancy. Shortly thereafter, it was official—they were an item.

It's said that Nancy was Frank's first serious girlfriend, and as such, he soon got to know not only Nancy but her whole family. Her home had many relatives coming in and out, and Frank enjoyed their lively dinner conversations and the general homey environment. As much as he wanted to be an adult and strike out on his own, the comforts of a traditional home were still quite a draw to him at this age. The emotional support during this transitionary period was crucial, and it was to the sympathetic ears of his newfound girlfriend that Sinatra often spoke about his growing dreams of becoming a professional singer.

At summer's end, Frank went back to his parents' house, but he kept up his relationship with Nancy without a hitch by frequently going back and forth between his parents and Nancy's place. Nancy's father, Mike Barbato, soon grew weary of Frank hanging around and became concerned that the young man with dreams of superstardom was a hopeless romantic with no real direction in life. Mr. Barbato was a no-nonsense, hard worker who put in long hours on construction sites. He expected anyone who was serious about his daughter to have a solid line of work as well; singing for food, beer, and cigarettes—as Sinatra often did in those days—just wasn't going to cut it.

Thus, one day at the family dinner table, Mike asked Sinatra point-blank what his job prospects were. Frank informed Mike that he was going to be singing at the Cat's Meow that Friday. That was indeed his latest gig, so for Frank, that constituted his most recent employment. It was not what Mike wanted to hear, and breaking through the typical polite dinner side conversation, he told Frank that if he were going to continue to see his daughter, he would have to have some form of regular employment.

Sinatra then swallowed his pride and accepted an offer to work as a plasterer's assistant at a construction site in Jersey City. He lasted on the job for a little over two weeks. His work had always been mediocre, and Mike himself had to come over on occasion to redo it for him, but the end finally came when Frank simply stopped coming in. He was fired after being a no-show for two straight days.

Sinatra was no doubt glad to be free of the daily grind that he had come to loathe so much, but he wasn't happy with the other direct consequence of his actions. Now, he was considered little more than a bum to Nancy's father, and he certainly wasn't welcome to come to their home any longer.

Chapter Four

Radio Debut

"I'm going to be the best singer in the world, . . . the best singer that ever was."

—Frank Sinatra

Kicked out of his second home, Frank was forced to meet up with his love interest Nancy away from her family. Since he didn't have his own place at the time, this usually meant that the couple would have to resort to make-out sessions in Frank's car after a night out on the town. The situation was not exactly ideal, and many evenings were punctuated by the sudden knocking on the windshield of a beat cop's billy club. Nevertheless, Sinatra persevered, and while he was pursuing Nancy, he also continued to pursue his dreams of full-on musical stardom.

It was around this time that he took part in an amateur contest at the State Theatre in Jersey City. He not only participated but made first place. Doors were suddenly opening for Sinatra, and shortly thereafter, in the spring of 1935, he was granted 15 minutes of precious airtime on a local radio station. Frank wouldn't be paid for his efforts, but just the idea of his voice being carried on the radio was enough at the time. He had grown up listening to his heroes on the radio, and now—at least in his mind—he was going to be one of them.

For his debut over the radio waves, Sinatra brought with him a good friend of his who played guitar, Matty Golizio. An adept and innovative guitarist, Matty would become a fixed feature of Sinatra's early career. There are no surviving records of how this session went, but according to some of the later testimony of his friends, it wasn't all that it was cracked up to be. His childhood friend Tony Macagnano, in fact, is said to have gotten on Frank's case about how bad he was. Tony allegedly told Frank afterward, "You'd better quit. Boy, you were terrible." It's hard to tell how good or bad Sinatra was, but whatever the case may be, he most certainly wasn't going to let the judgmental remarks of even his own close friends keep him down.

His mother, for one, had become a huge supporter. For most musicians, the idea that one's mother enjoyed their material wouldn't mean too much, but for Frank Sinatra, it meant a lot. Dolly was a socially active lady; she participated in local politics and knew quite a few people in different departments. It was through these connections that she got the ear of one Joseph Semperi, who ran the Union Club, an up-and-coming nightclub in the area. She was able to convince Semperi to give her son a full-time gig singing on his stage as part of the Union Club's entertainment.

It was a great opportunity for Sinatra to engage in some on-the-job training. Here, he was able to practice and refine his chops in front of a live audience, night after night. Frank appreciated the exposure, but it wasn't long before he wanted to move on to something bigger and better. He found it when he managed to get recruited for a local singing group called the Three Flashes. The now four-member group would eventually change their name to the Hoboken Four.

With this new group, Sinatra would make his way onto a local variety program called the *Major Bowes Amateur Hour*. The group's debut on the show was a stunning success. They managed to win first place and were given a six-month contract in which the band was sponsored to go on tour and make appearances on radio. It was also at this point that

Frank Sinatra became recognized as the group's frontman.

The tour was a demanding and financially draining affair. Although each band member was paid $75 a week (not bad for the 1930s) for their part in the tour, as the group traveled across 39 different states, they found that their funds were quite rapidly depleted. Nevertheless, they persevered, and by the time the group made their way to the west coast, Sinatra was already seen as a rising star. During one gig in Oakland, California, Frank was even asked to give a solo performance. Pushed to the sidelines, his band members were most likely equal parts jealous and in awe of how far Sinatra had come. They would later recall just how entranced the audience was when Frank sang.

All of this extra special attention often led to jealousy and arguments within the band, and during one such go-round, it's said that Frank got into a fistfight with fellow band member Fred Tamburro. As a result, Sinatra, apparently tired of the rivalry and confident that he could make it on his own, ended up quitting the tour early and heading back home.

The rest of the group did not fare too well without Frank and ultimately split apart as soon as the tour ended. The tour had been a frustrating affair for them, and most would give up on music shortly thereafter. For Frank Sinatra, however, the tour was not a disappointment at all but rather a revelation. He had experienced the thrill of being loved and admired on stage, and deep down, he knew that he had what it took to succeed.

Chapter Five

Arrest and Jail Time

"I'm for anything that gets you through the night—be it prayer, tranquilizers, or a bottle of Jack Daniels."

—Frank Sinatra

After returning from his tour with the Hoboken Four, Sinatra bounced around doing various singing gigs. He tried his luck as a singing waiter, and he performed off and on at Hoboken's Union Club. He also managed to get some airtime on local radio stations, such as the wide-ranging local outlet WAAT in Jersey City.

In 1937, Sinatra was able to get another big break when he was booked to appear on an NBC radio broadcast. He was by now getting bigger and better gigs and rubbing shoulders with the likes of Count Basie, Benny Goodman, Nat King Cole, and Billie Holiday. Even so, Frank felt like he had hit a slump and wasn't going anywhere. He was doing well enough on the local level, but he felt like he just couldn't get to the next step.

Dolly picked up on her son's mounting gloom and once again came to the rescue. She was able to use some of her many connections to get Frank a gig at a local club called the Rustic Cabin. Although the place had a western theme to it, it attracted a wide variety of talent. It also regularly drew large crowds. Most important to Sinatra was the fact that talent agents were frequently in the audience. Performing at the Rustic Cabin, Frank always made sure he was at his best since he never quite knew who might be listening to him sing.

Although Sinatra and his mother always insisted that it was Dolly's connections that helped get him the gig, some would later speculate that there were more sinister intermediaries at work. In particular, it would long be rumored that the Sinatras had connections to organized crime, and it was local mobsters who helped to open the door for Frank's music career. Frank himself always denied such claims, insisting that while he was aware of mobsters in the foreground of many of the circles he ran, he was not directly connected to them. The mob, after all, often ran legitimate businesses such as nightclubs, restaurants, and casinos as a front for their more illicit practices. Still, it certainly didn't help his case that his godfather, Willie Moretti, was a known underboss of the Genovese crime family.

At any rate, Sinatra got a gig at the Rustic Cabin as a singing waiter. Here, he not only sang but also had to serve food to patrons. It certainly wasn't the most ideal situation for him, considering his loathing of manual and repetitive labor, but the fact that he was able to sing seemed to make it worthwhile. The patrons of the Rustic Cabin, for their part, seemed to greatly enjoy Sinatra's dinnertime performances—an admiration that proved quite profitable when it came to tips. Sinatra was regularly able to cash in, as patrons handed over tons of extra money to show their gratitude. Frank Sinatra may have been a lowly singing waiter, but it didn't matter; if he was going to sing at all, he was always going to sing his heart out. It was clear to anyone who was paying attention that he sang with a true passion.

Sinatra's growing notoriety was, however, putting a strain on his relationship with his girlfriend, Nancy Barbato. By now, the budding singer had engaged in several flings with other women he had picked up while performing at the Rustic Cabin. Frank, it seems, had given up on any notion of going steady with his old sweetheart in preference for the opportunity to sow some wild oats. By the spring of 1938, he had met a new woman that he would become heavily involved with, Antoinette Della Penta, or as she was better known around town, "Toni."

At 27, Toni was a little older than Frank, and he was charmed by her beauty and sophistication. His mother, Dolly, however, was not too thrilled. Just one look at Toni had her hissing to Frank that his new girlfriend was nothing but "cheap trash." Dolly was known to be quite vocal, and she didn't shy away from speaking her mind, no matter whose feelings might be hurt. Frank, for his part, just brushed it off. He was infatuated with the lady and wanted to see more of her.

Toni was not as forward as some of the other women that Frank had been seeing and did not want to get too intimate with him unless she knew that they were in a committed and serious relationship. Frank soothed her concerns by proposing marriage. In 1938, He brought forth a ring and informed Toni of his intention to marry her. It was apparently after this engagement was made that Toni agreed to take their relationship to the next level.

Soon, the couple began staying at local hotels together, where Frank would sign them in as "Mr. and Mrs. Sinatra." Yet as many heartbroken people might attest, just because a person agrees to become engaged does not always mean they will follow through and get married. To Toni's distress, when she found out that she was pregnant, he began to distance himself from her. Toni then revealed that she had miscarried, and Frank, apparently thinking he was off the hook, dropped her completely. One can only imagine how hurtful all of this was to Toni. Frank had smooth-talked her into getting seriously involved with him by promising marriage, and then, once he got what he wanted, he jumped ship.

In truth, Frank was still seeing Nancy Barbato at the time, and even while he was sweet-talking Toni with marriage, he was saying much the same thing to Nancy, who had been patiently waiting for Frank to be hers and hers alone. Frank was two-timing the women and, making matters worse, both of them frequented the Rustic Cabin to hear Frank sing. Things then came to a head one night when Nancy was in attendance and took a phone call for Frank.

Frank was no doubt busy singing, and Nancy was kind enough to take calls for him. She wasn't too thrilled to hear who was on the other line—it was Toni Della Penta asking for Frank. Nancy was immediately enraged at the idea of another woman asking to speak to her man, and without any consideration of the pain that Frank had caused Toni, the conversation quickly devolved into a shouting match between the two. This then led to an infuriated and desperate Toni showing up at the club to confront both Frank and Nancy. Nancy and Toni then got into it and created a terrible scene. Their war of words got physical, and Toni started ripping at

Nancy's dress as if she wanted to tear it apart.

Sinatra, rather than intervening, tried to head for the exit when Toni chased after him and gave him a piece of her mind. It's not clear exactly what was said, but eventually, she angrily made her exit from the Rustic Cabin. This would not be the end of this matter, and Frank's cheating ways would have some real-world consequences. On November 26, 1938, Toni went so far as to file criminal charges against him. The charge was listed as "seduction under the promise of marriage."

Although there is no such law on the books in the modern age, back in the 1930s, there was indeed real legal recourse for a woman who felt that she had been wronged by a man who had seduced her with the promise of marriage. According to that standard, by all accounts, Sinatra was indeed guilty as charged because he did seduce Toni into intimacy with the promise that he would soon marry her.

At any rate, Frank Sinatra was arrested and thrown in jail shortly thereafter. It was then up to Dolly to bail her boy out once again.

Chapter Six

First Marriage

"A man doesn't know what happiness is until he's married. By then, it's too late."

—Frank Sinatra

Dolly Sinatra was absolutely horrified when her son was thrown in jail. Although Dolly was a woman with a lot of connections due to her political and social work in the community, rather than take a strong-arm approach, she first tried the personal touch. She sent her husband Marty over to Toni's father in the hopes that Marty might be able to reason with him and convince him of the need to have Toni drop the charges.

Marty was indeed convincing enough, not because he tried to intimidate or bully anyone, but rather because of the sympathetic figure that he cast. For anyone who saw him, it was rather clear that Marty was a man who was controlled by his wife. Dolly barked orders, and Marty obeyed. Marty probably didn't want to confront Toni's father, but he couldn't refuse an order, so there he was, looking sad and miserable, practically begging Toni's father to intervene.

Feeling sorry for the old man, Toni's father was soon on Marty's side, and both men were pleading with Toni to drop the charges against Frank and call the whole thing off. Yet Toni, who was still incredibly frustrated with Frank, wouldn't budge. Frank, in the meantime, was temporarily allowed to go home when his $1,500 bond was raised.

It was shortly after his release from jail that it came to light that Toni Della Penta was not quite the saint that she made herself out to be. Her divorce from a former husband had not been finalized, and as such, she was technically still married herself when she was seeing Frank. It was due to these findings that the charges against Sinatra were tossed out.

Nevertheless, it wasn't long before Toni struck again. She filed new charges against Frank, this time accusing him of adultery. It's kind of a tricky thing to consider her charging him with adultery since her own divorce from her previous husband had not yet been finalized, but she was apparently able to accuse Frank of as much since he was indeed seeing two girls at the same time. Again, this is an outdated charge which would not even be considered a crime today, but antiquated or not,

Sinatra was indeed arrested for the charge. He was then bailed out by Dolly a second time. In the end, though, Toni decided to drop the latest round of charges.

Although Frank ultimately escaped being convicted of any crime, his public and personal reputation took a hit. Frank Sinatra, the singing waiter, was by no means famous at this point in his career, but the papers still managed to pick up the story in their gossip columns. The tale was tawdry enough to get traction on the local level, and one newspaper, in particular, ran a story about it titled "Songbird Held on Morals Charge."

In a fury, Sinatra called up the paper and threatened to storm into the newsroom and attack those who wrote and published the story. He could vent his rage at the local press all he wanted, but one person he offended whom he could not throw a tantrum with was his long-time girlfriend, Nancy Barbato. She was now mortified to not only have absolute proof of Frank's infidelity but to have the details of it spread all over town. Sinatra couldn't scream at Nancy to make his shame go away. Instead, with his head down and a heavy heart, he had to plead for her forgiveness. He also promised her that it "would never happen again," and in order to show how serious he was, he proposed marriage—and this time, he meant it.

On February 4, 1939, standing in Jersey City's Our Lady of Sorrows Church, Mr. and Mrs. Sinatra were made man and wife. Nancy, who was walked down the aisle by her father— the same man who had previously looked down on Frank's musical ambition—was in tears. Her tears are said to have been tears of joy. Frank, on the other hand, might have been crying tears of another variety. Although Nancy would later claim that Frank was quite happy, his face was stoic at the time. An acquaintance of his—Marion Brush—who was at the wedding reception would later recall that Sinatra "looked like the saddest man."

In consideration of Frank's emotive capacity, it could be possible that he projected happiness to Nancy while giving sidelong, baleful glances to old friends like Marion. Perhaps this was what created such drastically different interpretations of his temperament at the time. The truth was that Sinatra was highly conflicted about the whole thing. He obviously cared about Nancy, and he had been pursuing her for quite a while. As such, he was happy to cement his relationship with her. Still, a part of him was also no doubt sad and full of trepidation at the prospect of putting away his old life with the finality of marital vows.

Nevertheless, Frank did seem to make the best of it, and after the wedding, he helped Nancy decorate their new Jersey City apartment. It's said that he picked out the curtains and generally helped Mrs. Sinatra make the place feel like home. Frank was also able to get a raise for his singing waiter gig at the Rustic Cabin and was now getting paid $25 a week plus tips. Such wages weren't too bad back then, but the newlyweds still often found themselves struggling financially. Nancy decided to help out by getting a job as a secretary. Sinatra would later recall that she worked during the day, and he worked at night, making it almost impossible for them to see each other on a regular basis.

During those first few years of marriage, events on the world stage began to take precedence in just about everyone's minds. Nazi Germany had risen to prominence and had made several land grabs in Europe. Many of these acquisitions were ignored, prompting the Germans to make even more trespasses. It was only when the Nazis stormed into

Poland in November of 1939 that world leaders finally realized they had to act, and World War II began. The U.S. would not enter the war until late 1941 when Germany's partner Japan bombed Pearl Harbor, but even so, the dark clouds that hung over Europe were already casting a long shadow over America. Frank Sinatra himself would soon be personally affected by the international storm that was brewing.

Chapter Seven

First Hit Song

"The best revenge is massive success."

—Frank Sinatra

By 1939, Frank Sinatra was growing weary of his gig as a singing waiter and was looking for a way out. One day he ran into the famed big band leader Glenn Miller and practically begged him to find him some more meaningful work. Miller was ambivalent, but one of his musical peers—Harry James—frequented the Rustic Cabin and began to show some interest. He recruited the then 23-year-old Frank Sinatra to sing for his band called the Music Makers. For this gig, Frank would get paid a whopping $75 a week. These dividends tripled what he typically made as a singing waiter for the Rustic Cabin. Sinatra jumped at the chance.

With the full force of a big band behind him, Sinatra's vocalizations were able to make leaps and bounds, reaching audiences like never before. During the summer, Frank and the Music Makers were out on tour and played a memorable show at the Panther Room in Chicago. In attendance was a local reporter by the name of James Bacon. Bacon would later describe how the audience was absolutely mesmerized by Sinatra's voice even though his frame "was so skinny, the microphone almost obscured him."

Skinny or not, this wiry young singer was ready to take things to the next level. That July, he went into the studio with the Music Makers to record some tracks. After the recording sessions wrapped up, the band continued their tour. It was while performing with the band in Chicago that Sinatra crossed paths with a man who would change his life forever— Tommy Dorsey.

Dorsey's long-time vocalist Jack Leonard had recently quit, and the band was looking for a full-time singer. In the middle of their search, Dorsey happened to hear Sinatra perform in Chicago. He thought that Frank just might be a good fit. He ended up having Sinatra audition for him, and pleased with what he heard, he recruited him to join his band. This, of course, meant that Sinatra would have to part ways with the Music Makers. Fortunately, he had become thoroughly disenchanted with them by this time, so it wasn't all that hard for him to cut ties with his former bandmates. They had helped him out of his singing waiter monotony and had taken him so far, but now they were as good as dead weight as far as Sinatra was concerned. They were holding him back, and he had to seize this new opportunity before it passed him by.

Sinatra was good enough to tell Harry James his plans face to face and braced himself for emotional blowback. But none came. Harry was, in fact, happy for him and wished him the best. Sinatra then jumped ship and was officially on tour with Dorsey and company.

It's a little unclear when Frank Sinatra first performed with Dorsey, but by

January of 1940, he was on stage in Indianapolis, Indiana, at the Lyric Theatre. He opened the act with a number called "Stardust," and the crowd was sucked right in. Sinatra loved every minute of it. He felt like he had died and gone to heaven that night. It was so unreal that Sinatra is said to have looked in a mirror afterward and gave himself a good pinch as if to make sure that he wasn't dreaming.

Sinatra was not only a hit with the audience, but he was also a hit with Dorsey himself. Although Dorsey was about ten years older than him, they became good friends, and Sinatra looked up to the man like a brother or even a father figure. Aiding their relationship was the fact that they were both night owls. Long after everyone else had gone to sleep, Sinatra and Dorsey would be up drinking and playing cards and simply having great conversations about all the things they had done and still wanted to do in life.

Frank also saw Tommy Dorsey as a mentor and credited him with helping to refine his abilities as a vocalist, or as he himself once unabashedly put it, "Tommy taught me everything I know about singing." It's interesting to think about an instrumentalist like Dorsey teaching Sinatra the finer points of singing, but such remarks weren't just flattery on Frank's part. It was Tommy's ability to sustain notes on his instrument and his sense of rhythm and phrasing with his horn that aided Sinatra's own sense of timing and style. With Dorsey's expertise in the foreground, Frank Sinatra recorded what would become his first hit song, a piece called "Polka Dots and Moonbeams."

Even while Sinatra was refining his art, his family life was moving on without him. His wife had already been pregnant when he went on the road, and it was while Frank was out on tour with Dorsey that his wife would give birth to their first child, a daughter named after her mother, Nancy Sandra Sinatra. Little Nancy was born on June 8, 1940. Frank was thrilled to be a father, and of course, he couldn't help but name Tommy Dorsey—the man who, at this point, he practically credited for his entire reason for being—as the child's godfather.

Chapter Eight

Sinatra during World War II

"People often remark that I'm pretty lucky. Luck is only important in so far as getting the chance to sell yourself at the right moment. After that, you've got to have talent and know how to use it."

—Frank Sinatra

In the fall of 1940, Sinatra was riding high. He was part of a dynamic band, had hits on the radio, and was a father to a beautiful baby girl. Regardless of his personal happiness, though, the world outside seemed as if it were about to come undone. With German tanks bulldozing through Europe, Italian troops laying claim to North Africa, and the Japanese doing their best to conquer the Pacific, it did indeed seem that the entire world was at war.

The United States would delay its entry into World War II for another year, but even so, it was already demanding that young American men sign up to be drafted for when that day would arrive. Sinatra himself would ultimately be classified as 4-F, or not acceptable for military service, due to a perforated eardrum (which he had sustained at birth). U.S. Army files also mentioned that the singer was "not acceptable material from a psychiatric viewpoint," although this was not made official at the time.

Sinatra's deferment would long foster resentment among other young men who served. Nevertheless, by this time, Sinatra had another hit song on the radio called "I'll Never Smile Again." This sentimental piece gained traction overseas and might as well have been a theme song for gloomy, war-worried western Europeans. As British Prime Minister Winston Churchill himself once told Sinatra, "You belong to my people as well as your own. For yours was the voice that sang them to sleep in that infamous summer of 1940."

That fall, in the meantime, Sinatra was given a small role in a film called *Las Vegas Nights*, in which he was able to sing his newest hit. During this stint in Hollywood, Frank had one of what would be many extramarital affairs, as he lived it up in California with an actress by the name of Alora Gooding.

After the filming was over, Sinatra said his goodbyes to Alora and thought that would be the end of it, but shortly after his return home to his wife Nancy, Frank's escapades would come back to haunt him. While Sinatra was asleep, Nancy looked through her husband's wallet. Inside she found a photo of Alora. Frank had snapped the photo himself, and the girl in the image had an alluring smile on her face as if she were enticing the cameraman. With her blood pressure rising at the sight, Nancy knew something was up and immediately questioned Frank about who the girl in the picture was.

Sinatra was no doubt startled but quickly produced a lie he thought would satisfy her. He shrugged the whole thing off as just a fan who had happened to give him her picture.

Nancy wasn't buying it, and as she stared him down, she forced him to repeat the lie once again, as Frank even more forcefully insisted that it was just a photo some fan had given him. Nancy was disturbed, but with enough cajoling from her husband, she finally let the matter rest, and Nancy, Frank, and their daughter went on to have a relatively happy Christmas together.

Shortly after they rang in the new year of 1941, Frank Sinatra was back in the studio recording music with the band. As he was crafting more hit songs, the main draw increasingly became Sinatra, while Dorsey and his band faded into the background. This fundamental shift was evident when the band went on tour in the summer of 1941, and Sinatra was greeted by throngs of female fans who screamed his name out loud. Sinatra couldn't help but realize that he was the star of the show—with or without Dorsey and company.

Dorsey saw the writing on the wall as well, and in January of 1942, he gave Frank the go-ahead to log studio time as a solo artist. As a result, Sinatra recorded the tracks "Night and Day," "The Song Is You," "The Night We Called it a Day," and "The Lamplighter's Serenade." Sinatra then went on tour with the group for the last time that summer. He would continue his rise over the next few years with more hits and engage in more wide-ranging tours that would make him an international icon. He became so popular, in fact, that during a gig on October 11, 1944 (Columbus Day), his fans were so excited they caused a riot, an incident that would go down in history as the "Columbus Day Riot." Twenty years before Beatlemania, the world was being shaken by Sinatra-mania.

Sinatra made many notable recordings during this period, including "She's Funny That Way" and

"Embraceable You." With popular songs on the radio and sold-out concerts, Frank was really raking in the dough. Rather than the chump change he had been given in the past, from 1944 to 1945, it's said that Sinatra netted a whopping 1.4 million dollars, which would amount to tens of millions today. Needless to say, Sinatra and his family were soon leaving their cramped apartment in Jersey City behind for good.

Before long, they moved out west to a luxurious home in California's San Fernando Valley. It was a step up for sure, but Nancy had a hard time adjusting to the change in lifestyle, and she and Frank were frequently getting into arguments. Even so, the couple would patch things up well enough to have two more children together—Frank Jr. in 1944 and Tina in 1948. In the long run, though, the strain on the Sinatra marriage from incessant bickering and Frank's philandering would ultimately prove to be their undoing.

Chapter Nine

Late Life and Death

"I would like to be remembered as a man who had a wonderful time living life, a man who had good friends, fine family—and I don't think I could ask for anything more than that."

—Frank Sinatra

In 1945, just as the victory of the Allied forces was all but assured, Frank Sinatra made his way to a stage in Europe to do a show for the army. Frank, who had received a deferment, had long been dogged for not donning a uniform and serving alongside all the other young men his age who had been put on the front lines. The fact that he waited until the enemy had been beaten to a standstill and it was perfectly safe to land in Europe only made his detractors criticize him even more.

Nevertheless, in the year following the war, in 1946, his album *The Voice of Frank Sinatra* sold like hot cakes and reached the number one slot on the charts. His 1947 album—*Songs by Sinatra*—did equally well. But it was perhaps his 1948 attempt to make a Christmas album—*Christmas Songs by Sinatra*—that would prove to be one of his most memorable efforts.

Songs like "Have Yourself a Merry Little Christmas" continue to be played every year without fail and, despite the changes and evolutions of the genre, never seem to lose their charm. A song such as this captures Sinatra's thoughtful, wistful nature. He seems somewhat sad yet hopeful as he encourages the listener to "let your heart be light." In many ways, Frank Sinatra was one of the first artists to show a vulnerable side. His fans sensed the raw emotion in his voice and felt as though he was sharing a part of his soul with them. A song like "Have Yourself a Merry Little Christmas" did indeed do a great job of capturing Frank's ability to do so.

Many would argue that this Christmas album captured Frank Sinatra at the top of his game. Like all icons, Sinatra would soon learn that as easily as one rose, they could just as easily begin to fall. His 1949 follow-up—*Frankly Sentimental*—just didn't seem to capture the same magic that had made him so endearing in the past.

Sinatra's personal reputation also began to take a hit as his extramarital affairs became more widely known. In particular, it was his ongoing fling with Ava Gardner that began to attract a lot of attention in the press. Frank would ultimately leave his wife for Gardner, marrying her in 1951. Yet although

Frank and Ava were deeply attracted to each other initially, their relationship would be a stormy one throughout.

Just as Frank Sinatra's star continued to dim in the early 1950s, there was a new star that began to rise. In 1954, Elvis Presley popularized the new sounds of rock and roll. During this period, Sinatra, discouraged with the fading interest in his music, switched gears and began to try his luck in film. It was around this time that he starred in the epic *From Here to Eternity*. Here, Sinatra played the role of a U.S. soldier stationed in Hawaii just prior to the Japanese attack on Pearl Harbor. Although he hadn't served during the war, Frank was able to realistically portray the life of a military man on the big screen and won an Academy Award for his efforts.

Sinatra followed up his work on *From Here to Eternity* with another film called *The Man with the Golden Arm.* In this movie, Frank played the role of an ex-con and drug addict, struggling to get his head straight. Demonstrating his ability to portray the dark side of life, Sinatra once again knocked it out of the park, and the huge box office returns stood as a testament to that fact. He was also nominated for another Oscar award.

Sinatra then managed to fuse his acting and musical abilities by making a successful go in the musical *Guys and Dolls* in 1955 before starring in *High Society* in 1956, which had him sharing the screen with the likes of Bing Crosby, Grace Kelly, and Louis Armstrong. In 1957, Frank starred in the comedy *Pal Joey* for which he was awarded a Golden Globe Award for Best Actor.

While Sinatra was enjoying popular acclaim as an actor, his marriage to Ava Gardner had become irreparably strained, and the couple permanently called it quits in that very year. Their time together had been passionate but volatile from the beginning, with many ups and downs. Divorce was never far from either of their lips during their short marriage, so it didn't come as much of a surprise when it finally happened in 1957. Nevertheless, the two would remain friends despite the emotional turmoil they had gone through.

Shortly after, Sinatra would make a musical comeback by forging a music super-group called the Rat Pack. Here, he performed alongside Dean Martin, Peter Lawford, Sammy Davis Jr., and Joey Bishop. It was a successful run while it lasted. Much of the 1960s for Sinatra must have seemed like a blur. Although middle-aged at this point in his life, he was running full steam ahead. He would marry actress Mia Farrow in 1966, whom he would then divorce two years later.

As his life continued to fly by, both on a musical as well as a personal level, Sinatra seemed as if he was struggling to get his footing. He was becoming more politically active, supporting the civil rights movement as well as Jewish causes, but all the while drinking heavily and taking powerful antidepressants. By the end of the decade, he was trying his luck once again in film, and in 1967, he played the role of a hard-nosed detective in *Tony Rome.* The film was a hit and would be followed by an encore performance in *Lady Cement* in 1968. Sinatra's film career would flop in 1970, however, with *Dirty Dingus Magee.* The film was meant to be a comedy, but instead of laughing at the antics of the actors, most viewers laughed at how horrible the movie was.

Sinatra made another musical comeback in the meantime, with his 1973 album titled with precisely this very intention in mind. It was called *Ol' Blue Eyes Is Back.* The album did well enough, ranking high on the charts. In order to support the album, Sinatra engaged in extensive touring in 1974, which took him all over America, Europe, and Asia.

Along with his musical career, Sinatra also reprised his personal life, marrying his love interest Barbara Marx in 1976. It was his fourth marriage, but this one was built to last. Frank would remain with Barbara for the rest of his days. The following year, Sinatra's world was rocked by the death of his mother, Dolly. It's hard for anyone to have a parent perish, but Frank's case was especially difficult because she did not die of old age or any other naturally occurring ailment. Dolly died in a plane crash, and even worse, her plane crashed while she was en route to pay him a visit. Sinatra was absolutely devastated at the loss. Nevertheless, he knew the show had to go on, and he continued his run at Caesars Palace in Las Vegas over the next few years.

After a period of reflection, Sinatra managed to compose a new album in 1980 called *Trilogy: Past Present Future*. The album was generally well-received, and he followed this up with his 1981 album *She Shot Me Down*. This record didn't do quite as well commercially but managed to garner a strong cult following all the same. By 1982, Sinatra was back in his old stomping grounds in Las Vegas. He was a staple of the city at this point and signed a multi-million-dollar deal with the Golden Nugget casino and resort. He was contracted to remain a regular presence for the next few years.

Things were going well enough for Sinatra in the 1980s, but in 1986, he faced a health scare during a performance at the New Jersey resort town of Atlantic City. He found out he was suffering from diverticulitis, an inflammation of the large intestine, and had to have surgery. After he recovered, Sinatra was back on top of things, embarking on a tour with his old Rat Pack chums before returning to the studio to record a new album.

Frank Sinatra embarked on several solo tours in the early 1990s until his health once again began to decline in 1994. Deciding to take it easy, he gave what would be his last live performance on February 25, 1995. Sinatra turned 80 years old that year and was now ready to retire for good.

Conclusion

After leaving it all behind and retiring from show business at age 80, Sinatra only had a couple of years left to sit back and reflect on his life. He and his wife relocated from their old home in Palm Springs to Los Angeles. Frank had two houses in LA at the time—a sprawling mansion in Beverly Hills as well as a house on Malibu Beach. It was at the Our Lady of Malibu Church that Frank and his wife Barbara would celebrate their 20th wedding anniversary. Although this was a time of celebration, it was also becoming increasingly clear that their remaining time together was growing short. In

November, Sinatra suffered from a heart attack and had to go to the hospital. This was the first of two heart attacks; he wouldn't survive the second one.

On May 14, 1998, an 82-year-old Frank Sinatra finally succumbed to a fatal cardiac episode. His funeral was held just days later, on May 20, and hundreds of friends, family, and admirers were in attendance. Beyond those there that day for his funeral, there was a whole world of people out there who mourned the loss of one of the greatest performers in modern history. Ol' Blue Eyes was gone, but he most certainly was not forgotten.

Bibliography

Ackelson, Richard W. (1992). *Frank Sinatra: A Complete Recording History of Techniques, Songs, Composers, Lyricists, Arrangers, Aessions, and First-issue Albums, 1939–1984.*

Dwiggins, Don (2016). *Frankie: The Life and Loves of Frank Sinatra.*

Fuchs, Jeanne & Prigozy, Ruth (2007). *Frank Sinatra: The Man, the Music, the Legend.*

Kaplan, James (2010). *Frank: The Voice.*

Kuntz, Tom & Kuntz, Phil (2000). *The Sinatra Files: The Secret FBI Dossier.*

Summers, Anthony & Swan, Robbyn (2010). *Sinatra: The Life.*

Printed in Poland
by Amazon Fulfillment
Poland Sp. z o.o., Wrocław
21 July 2023

c24bd05c-412e-4ef3-a1cd-4f353fa8a8bdR01